Best Wishes Honey.

Aug 24 /83

Love. Bobbie

A Sketchbook of Birds

C. F. Tunnicliffe R.A.
A Sketchbook of Birds
Introduction by Ian Niall

HOLT, RINEHART AND WINSTON
NEW YORK

First published in the United States of America in 1979
by Holt, Rinehart and Winston, 383 Madison Ave., New York, N.Y. 10017.

Library of Congress Cataloging in Publication Number: 79-1920
ISBN: 0-03-052326-5

Printed in Italy

10 9 8 7 6 5 4 3 2 1

Contents

Publisher's Note

The sketches reproduced in this book are taken from seventeen sketchbooks filled by the artist between 1934 and 1962. Some of the larger sketches have been slightly reduced in order to fit the page.

Most of the sketches were made at two locations: the island of Anglesey, where Charles Tunnicliffe lived from 1947 until his death in February 1979, and the country near Macclesfield in Cheshire, where he spent the first twenty-odd years of his life, and frequently re-visited.

In nearly all cases, Tunnicliffe noted on his sketches the location and the date of composition; the year of composition and the scientific names of the birds have been added in the captions.

The publisher acknowledges with gratitude the unfailing assistance of the artist's sister, Mrs Dorothy Downes, and of Mr and Mrs Ian Niall, without whom the book could not have been published.

Sadly, Charles Tunnicliffe did not live to see publication of this book, but he saw colour proofs of some of the pictures and took pleasure in discussing and corresponding about publishing details during the planning stages. His last letter, giving details of his early wood-engravings, was received at the Gollancz office on the day of his death.

Introduction
by Ian Niall

In popular imagination a romantic aura surrounds the lives of artists, but I have always believed that any artist who is more than a nine days' wonder must have an essentially practical approach. Great talent is cultivated in interminable days, in years of striving to master a technique, in applying continually a special imagination, which is the artist's gift.

Charles Tunnicliffe, the son of ordinary farming folk from Cheshire, was a man whose application, whose undaunted perseverance, put my own rather superficial approach to most things in shameful shade.

I first knew of him (in common with thousands of others) as the illustrator of Henry Williamson's famous books *Tarka the Otter* (1932) and *Salar the Salmon* (1935). Before this, Tunnicliffe had sold some superb etchings while still a student at the Royal College of Art. Most went into private collections, but some were purchased by the Victoria and Albert Museum in London and the National Gallery, Stockholm. He was quickly making his name as an engraver and illustrator of the first rank, and his work for Williamson was the prelude to a lifetime of illustrating books for authors small and great (Hemingway, Negley Farson, H. E. Bates and Richard Church among them). To all of these, and to many others, Tunnicliffe brought something exceptional, an uncanny sensitivity, the ability to enter the author's fantasy – the mark of the great illustrator.

Twelve or thirteen years ago I met Charles Tunnicliffe for the first time. His home on the island of Anglesey was not far from mine above Llandudno in North Wales. We began to correspond, and to meet from time to time and I formed the idea that I might one day write about his life and art. Although I am neither an ornithologist nor a student of art, I felt that I might bring a certain understanding to the task. We came from similar backgrounds. Eventually I decided to put away other work and prepare a biography. Charles greeted my proposal diffidently (being the most modest of men) but agreed to see me each week. We talked about his early life in Macclesfield, his struggles to make a living as an artist, his marriage, his experiences with the highly inflammable Henry Williamson. Throughout, he would punctuate any reminiscence with amazingly wide ranging observations on birds and animals. For me, our meetings were far more than nostalgia; I was sitting at the feet of a great naturalist and a great observer. Charles had studied birds with an artist's, not a shooting man's, eye. He knew the golden plover's flight, the juvenile plumage of the rare northern variety, the feeding rituals of falcons and cormorants, the precise extent of a snowy owl's wing. This vast knowledge was recorded in his field notes and sketchbooks, an amazing collection of the most detailed study and the finest art in themselves.

As the pages of my notes increased, I felt that it was time to look for a publisher. My friend and fishing companion, David Burnett of Victor Gollancz, needed no second invitation to come up from London and talk about the book with Charles and myself. When he arrived at my house I proceeded to talk him into the ground about *The Life and Art of Charles Tunnicliffe*. On the journey over to Anglesey he kept falling asleep as I continued at length to describe the marvels that Tunnicliffe had shown me, including his drawings for the original wood-engravings for *Tarka*, and his extraordinary 'bird maps', large scale detailed studies of hundreds of birds, some of which I thought might go into my book. On arriving at Shorelands, the house at Malltraeth where Tunnicliffe lived for thirty years, we looked together at the 'bird maps' and then I once again took up with Charles the thread of our previous discussion. My publishing friend had fallen into a kind of reverie over some sketchbooks he had found casually stowed in a cupboard. It seemed to me that he was pondering technical problems. I was afraid that he would say that my book could not be illustrated in the generous way I had hoped. Suddenly he remarked that here was treasure trove. Tunnicliffe's bird sketches were something the world must see. There was nothing like them. They called for the finest possible reproduction, paper and printing. Everyone who loved beautiful work would want to possess a book of the sketches, as a boy wants to keep the exotic butterfly he cups in his hands. Bird-watchers, ornithologists and artists would all be enchanted by it. Tunnicliffe blinked for a moment and smiled at this enthusiasm. In a long life dedicated to his art he had accumulated so much work of such breath-taking quality that he thought no more about it, but we were thinking about it and the need to let the world see it. Would he entrust the priceless sketchbooks to the publisher's care for a while so that the pictures could be photographed? Tunnicliffe had a generous nature and he graciously agreed. And so *A Sketchbook of Birds* was born.

Tunnicliffe's *alter ego* was art. In the face of this unturnable force, his parents accepted that their son must be allowed to cultivate his talent and could not remain to help them on the farm. He went, first by one scholarship to Macclesfield School of Art and then by another to the Royal College of Art. From there he proceeded to exhibit at and then to be admitted to the Royal Academy. In 1977, towards the end of a great career, his name appeared in the Queen's Birthday Honours List. Along the way, and in the course of the busiest lifetime any artist can ever have had, he amassed sketches – some of the best of which are published here. Charles Tunnicliffe's *Sketchbook of Birds* speaks for itself. Writing an introduction to it, I know that my words will be read not before but after the reader has turned the pages in wonder, over and over again.

Tunnicliffe's place in art is assured by virtue of endless work at the easel and drawing board. My problem is to find words to put upon it – obsession, perfectionism, meticulous care, beauty. I remember Charles once quoting me the favourite tag of one of his professors at the Royal Academy one day when we were talking about the nature of art – 'Tell me where is fancy bred, or in the heart or in the head?' There is no answer, but fancy – the conception of beauty – being there, Tunnicliffe fostered it when he could, to the exclusion of everything else, and for a life-time. People will go on collecting Tunnicliffe's prints, coveting those early etchings – *The Bull*, *The Cheshire Plain*, *A Winter Landscape* – coveting also the water-colours snatched up by eager buyers on the first day of the Academy exhibitions, long after most of his contemporaries are forgotten. If I commented further on the *Sketchbook of Birds* it would be to remind those who have seen it that they are enjoying a very privileged view of the quiet life of a private man – and a great artist.

Tan-yr-Allt Cottage
Llandudno, February 1979

Location Notes to the Sketches

The purpose of these brief notes is to enable the reader to locate on a map the sites referred to in Tunnicliffe's sketches. In a few cases, identification of the sites is uncertain. Most sites are either close to Macclesfield, the artist's home town in Cheshire, or on the island of Anglesey, where he made his home in 1947 and where he remained until his death.

Alderley Edge—Cheshire. To the north-west of Macclesfield.

Amlwch—ancient port in north Anglesey.

Anglesey—island situated off the north coast of Wales. First connected to the mainland by Thomas Telford's famous bridge across the Menai Strait.

Beaumaris—Anglesey, at the eastern end of the Menai Strait.

Birtles Pool—west of Macclesfield, in the grounds of Birtles Hall.

Bodorgan headland—south-west Anglesey, north of the Cefni estuary.

Bont Farm—near the artist's home, south-west Anglesey.

Bosley Reservoir—south of Macclesfield, by the A54 and A523 road junction.

Capesthorne Pool—west of Macclesfield in the grounds of Capesthorne Hall.

Cemlyn Lake—on the north coast of Anglesey, west of Amlwch.

Clitheroe—(Bradley Hall) Lancashire.

Clough Brook—a stream near the artist's birthplace, south of Macclesfield.

Cob Lake—by Malltraeth, Anglesey.

Crochan Caffo—a pool in the marshes near Llangaffo, Anglesey.

Dinas Point—by Bodorgan, off the northern shore of the Cefni estuary.

Foel Ferry—near the western end of the Menai Strait on the Anglesey side, opposite Caernarvon (the ferry no longer operates).

Foryd Estuary—North Wales, across the Menai Strait from Anglesey, at the western end.

Gawsworth Pool—south of Macclesfield in the grounds of Gawsworth Hall.

Glan Avon—probably Glanrafon, a farm near the artist's home in Anglesey.

Goldsitch Moss—country area to the south-east of Macclesfield.

Gull Island, Aberdaron—off the coast of north-west Wales. The two islands are usually called 'The Gwyllans'.

Handa Island, Sutherland—Scotland, off the north-west highland coast.

Hawk's-head Clough—near Higher Sutton, Macclesfield.

Iona—island off the south-west shore of Mull, north-west Scotland.

Kendal—south-west Lake District, Westmorland.

Llandwyn lighthouse—Llandwyn Island, south Anglesey, on the southern side of the Cefni estuary.

Lligwy Bay—on the north-east coast of Anglesey.

Llyn Coron—a small lake near Bodorgan railway station, south-west Anglesey.

Macclesfield—Cheshire. The artist's home town, just north of Langley, his birthplace.

Malltraeth Lake—near the artist's home, south-west Anglesey.

Moelfre—on the north-east coast of Anglesey.

Nant Bychan rocks—north-east coast of Anglesey, between Traeth Bychan and Moelfre.

Northwich—Cheshire. A small town to the west of Macclesfield.

Pont Aber Glaslyn—Snowdonia, North Wales, in the mountain pass south of Beddgelert (A498 road).

Porth Aber (usually Porth yr Aber)—near Moelfre on the east coast of Anglesey.

Radnor Mere—a lake south of Nether Alderley, to the north-west of Macclesfield.

Radnor Woods—beech woods south of Nether Alderley, to the north-west of Macclesfield.

Redesmere—a lake west of Macclesfield, Cheshire.

Shorelands—the artist's home by Malltraeth, south-west Anglesey.

South Stack—cliffs off the north-west coast of Holy Island, Anglesey.

Stack Rocks—A group of rocks in St Bride's Bay to the north-east of Skomer Island. In 1938 CFT and his wife were marooned on the island by bad weather for some days and were forced to live off seagull's eggs.

Traeth Bach—estuary in north-west Wales, south of Porthmadog.

Traeth Bychan—a small bay on the north-east coast of Anglesey, south of Moelfre.

Ty Gwyn—south of Cefni Reservoir, Llangefni, Anglesey.

Y Felin—literally 'The Mill', of which there are several near the artist's home on Anglesey. The precise location is unknown.

Seabirds

1 Common gull, *Larus canus,* on the island of Iona, Argyll, September 1934.
2 Great black-backed gull, *Larus marinus,* Iona, September 25th, 1934.
3 Young herring gull, *Larus argentatus,* Iona, September 1934.

adult

adult

Second year bird

Light grey markings of
sometimes fawnish
Winter plumage →

Sepia dark

Faun

Common Gull.
Sept: Iona.

First year bird.

I

Iona Sept. 25th
Gr Black-backed gull.

Seen singly. Sometimes with
a crowd of common gulls resting
on the machair. Today seen
feeding on the body of a dead
dog & thrown up at White Sands
bay. Two Hoody crows also feeding
with him.

Seen also in the pastures
behind the farms on rising
ground resting with a young
gull.

In Iona regarded as the king
of thieves and murderers.

From memory.

From life.

2

Young Herring gull.
Iona. Sept.

3

4 Studies of immature herring gull, *Larus argentatus*, Moelfre, September 1944.

5 Juvenile black-headed gulls, *Larus ridibundus*, near Beaumaris, July 13th, probably 1948.

June 13th On Sketch Book.

Scapulars darker grey than
wing coverts.
Slightly sepia

Tail pale grey
not grey white tip
Legs grey & feet.
Beak amber green
and yellowish
towards the tip.
Tube blackish.

Shag and well grown young still in down but with tail and wing quills
sprouting. Young often with open beak and its throat throbbing rapidly because
of the heat. Here it is lying with its left leg thrust back behind its
stumpy tail.
A view from above which accounts for the foreshortening of the adult.

Juvenile scrambling
about cliff face. It could
fly and later did so.
(this drawing from memory)

A worn bird with head paler
than back. Scapulars and wing
coverts a dirty sepia brown with
pale worn-brown edges.
Iris appeared pale yellow.

6 Fulmar, *Fulmarus glacialis*, near Stack Rock. June 13th, 1938.
7 Shags, *Phalacrocorax aristotelis*: adult with young, and juvenile. Bodorgan headland, May 1948.

8 Cormorant, *Phalacrocorax carbo*, nestling, Bodorgan headland, July 17th, 1949.
9 Puffins, *Fratercula arctica*, Gull Island, Aberdaron, July 30th, 1935.

9

June 2ⁿᵈ

Common Terns. Nant Bychan
Rocks.

One preening on a rock. Other
brought a fish to it but preening
bird ignored it and flew away.
Other bird at once swallowed fish.

10 Common terns, *Sterna hirundo*, one offering a fish. Nant Bychan rocks, June 2nd, 1942.

June 3rd Lligwy Bay.
Pair of Little Terns. Suspect they
are the same pair noted at Traeth
Bychan as they were at Lligwy
during high tide when all the sand
at Traeth Bychan is covered.

slight display and calling before flying off, after a stay with its mate

II

II Pair of little terns, *Sterna albifrons*, Lligwy Bay, June 3rd, 1942.

12 Oystercatchers, *Haematopus ostralegus,* on the rocks near Traeth Bychan, April 28th, 1946.

Two Great Black-backs swimming
at the edge of the weed. One holding
wings outside flank feathers.

13 Pair of great black-backed gulls, *Larus marinus*, 1944 or 1945.

may 19th Malltraeth
Lake.

Little Terns feeding from
lake and would rest in
groups on the mud in ear
with Dunlin and Common
Terns.

14

14 Little terns, *Sterna albifrons*, feeding and resting, Malltraeth Lake, May 19th, 1945.

15 Autumn sandwich terns, *Sterna sandvicensis*, and one common tern, Lligwy Bay, September 8th, 1944.

Sept 10. Nant Bychan Rocks. Evening.
Oystercatchers, Ring Plover and a Teal

the rising tide caused the birds to
take fresh positions periodically. Once
the Teal was awash but maintained
its footing on the weed covered rock. Later
it flew onto the sea ...

16

16 Oystercatchers, *Haematopus ostralegus*, ringed plover, *Charadrius hiaticula*, and a teal, *Anas crecca*, Nant Bychan rocks, evening, September 10th, 1944.

17 Juvenile guillemot, *Uria aalge*, changing to first winter plumage, October 2nd, 1948.

18 Razorbill, *Alca torda*, in winter plumage, probably autumn 1947.
19 Guillemots, *Uria aalge*, Handa Island, Sutherland, June 16th, 1939.

19

20 Common tern, *Sterna hirundo*, on rocks above Porth Aber, June 1942.

I

21 Common terns, *Sterna hirundo*, one presenting a fish, Amlwch, June 1942.

June 2nd   Amlwch Rocks
(Opposite Amlwch Island on which are
many Terns)

Common Terns. Facing a high wind. They often
spread their tails to preserve balance.

On the shelves of Amlwch Island they squatted close and looked like a mass of
fawl-gray eggs.

22

22 Common terns, *Sterna hirundo*, facing a high wind, Amlwch, June 2nd, 1942.
23 Studies of guillemots, *Uria aalge*, Stack Rock, June 12th, 1938.

Breeding breast feather

Landing.

Head dipping

Black-heads. Traeth Bychan. Sept 4th.
One with a very pronounced rosy breast and
undersides. Others with less noticeable rosy tin[g]

Traces of the black-brown
hood still to be seen in
this bird.

From memory

24

24 Autumn black-headed gulls, *Larus ridibundus*, and an immature herring gull, *Larus argentatus*,
Traeth Bychan, September 4th, 1944.
25 Black-headed gulls, *Larus ridibundus*, swimming, Iona, September 19th, 1934.

Black Headed Gull.
Sept. 19th IONA.

25

June 5ᵗ Nant Bychan
Rock

Turnstones. Small flock of 8 or 9.
One very fine cock bird among them.
Plumage of the others very varied
and confusing.

26

26 Turnstones, *Arenaria interpres*, at Nant Bychan rocks, June 5th, 1942.

Little Tern June 3rd 42
Traeth Bychan.
Again being fed by its mate which
on one occasion brought a bigger fish
than usual which the other bird at first
refused to touch. The hunter eventually persuaded
her to take it but had to kill the struggling fish before she would do so.

Lit by its evening sun. Looked very yellow.

27 Little tern, *Sterna albifrons*, in evening sunlight, Traeth Bychan, June 3rd, 1942.

28 Turnstones, *Arenaria interpres,* at Nant Bychan rocks, June 1942.

Resting pose

Interrupting Preening to watch me.

Resting

June 4th 42
Nant Bychan Rocks
This group not actually
seen but the various
poses noted in individual
birds as they rested singly on
the rocks

29 Oystercatchers, *Haematopus ostralegus,* at Nant Bychan rocks, June 4th, 1942.

30 Black-headed gulls, *Larus ridibundus,* showing variation in first summer plumage,
Malltraeth Lake, June 2nd, 1944.

Waders

31 Wood sandpiper, *Tringa glareola,* probably a juvenile, Cob Lake, August 20th, 1952.

august 20°. Ock Lake.
Wood Sandpiper. Probably a juvenile

Also seen up at Oct 15ᵗʰ on the shore

Oct. 5' Grey Plover on shore in front of the house. 1 in the morning
Feeding on worms 4 in the evening

32 Grey plover, *Pluvialis squatarola*, on the shore at Malltraeth, October 5th, 1950.

Curlew Sandpiper. Malltraeth Lake
First week in September. Usually not
Dunlin but occasionally in a flock
exclusively of C. Samples

33 Curlew sandpiper, *Calidris ferruginea*, Malltraeth Lake, September 1945.
34 Knot, *Calidris canutus*, feeding at Cob Lake, September 12th, 1952.
35 The same three knot, four days later.

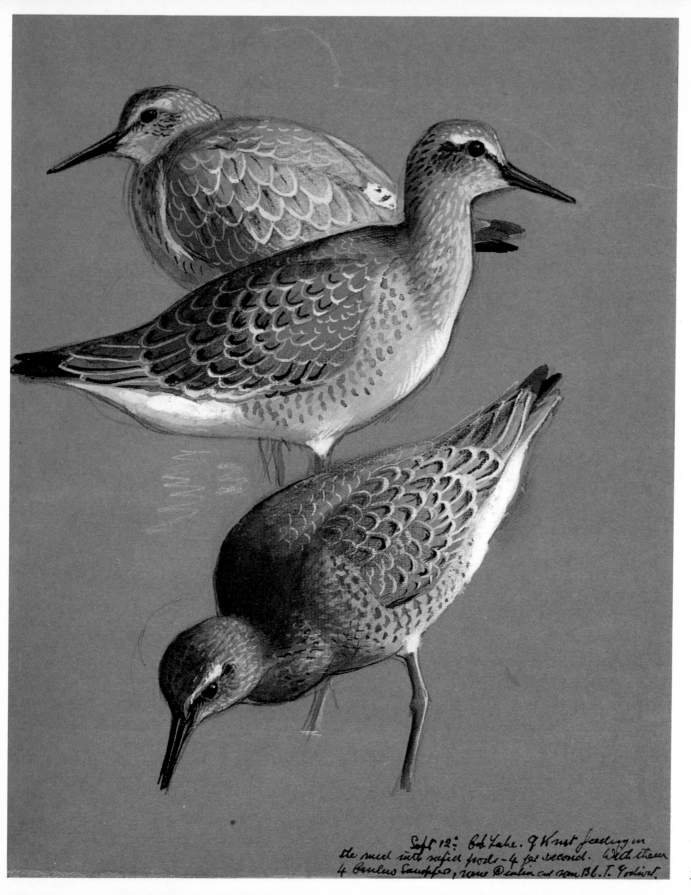

Sept 12:. Bob Lake. 9 Knot feeding in
the mud into rapid pools – 4 fee second. With these
4 Curlew Sandpipers, some Dunlin and some Bl.T. Godwit.

34

Sept. 16. 3 Knots in both Lake still
Also 1 Bar T. Godwit 6 B.T. Godwit. Many Dunlin.
3 Little Stints. 1 Greenshank. Herons Swans Gulls
(black headed) 1 Oyster catcher, Cormorant;
no Curlew Sandpiper Today.

aug 2nd. Jony Lapwing. N.B. under tail coverts casting of
above tail.

36 Studies of juvenile lapwing, *Vanellus vanellus*, August 2nd, 1948.

In some birds this pale margin to the mantle very indistinct.

May 18ᵗʰ Dunlin on the mud of Cob Lake.

37

37 Dunlin, *Calidris alpina,* in breeding plumage at Cob Lake, May 18th, 1949.

Ruff. Sept 9th.
A solitary bird on Malltraeth
Lake.

38

38 Solitary ruff, *Philomachus pugnax*, at Malltraeth Lake, September 9th, 1946.

Sept 8th Lligwy Beach.
Juvenile Sanderlings in a flock
of fifteen. feeding and sleeping on the
tide edge. Tide ebbing. General appearance Black Grey & White but one or two birds were buffish about the upper breast and shoulders.

39 Sanderlings, *Calidris alba*, at the tide edge, Lligwy Beach, September 8th, 1948.
40 Adult ruff, *Philomachus pugnax*, in moult. Two views of the same bird, Cob Lake, August 26th, 1952.
41 Curlew sandpipers, *Calidris ferruginea*, with a dunlin, *Calidris alpina*, (right centre) Cob Lake,
September 9th, 1952.

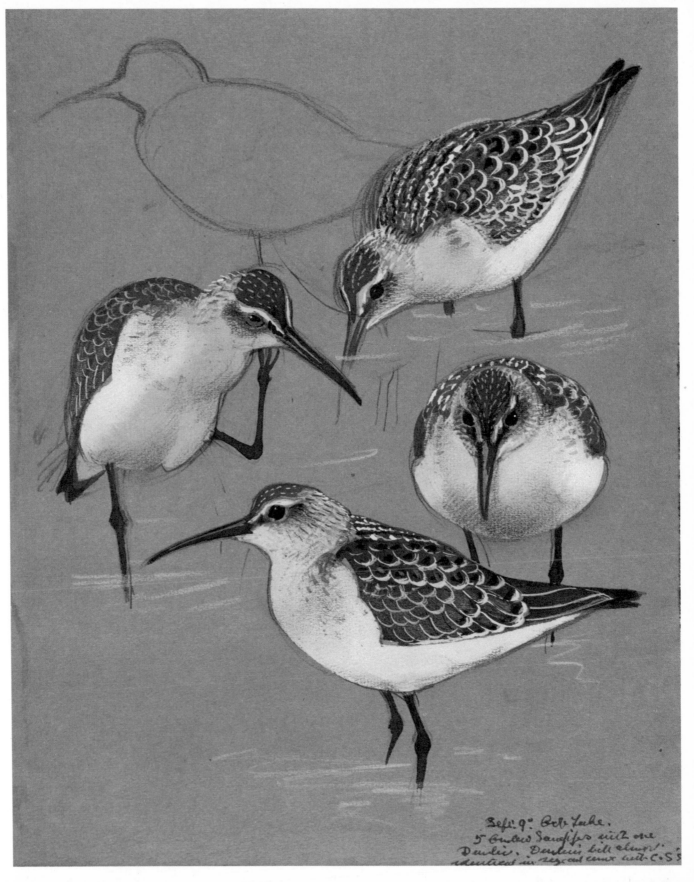

Sept 9th Colt Lake.
5 Curlew Sandpipers with one
Dunlin. Dunlin's bill almost
identical in general curve with C.S.S

Ruffs. Sept 2nd to Sept 10th
Malltraeth field pools. 5 has the greatest
number seen. Variation in size very apparent
the larger birds appearing more suffused with
warm buff, the smaller more black & white in
the lacing of the scapulars & wings

Will often stand more
erect than this

42

42 Ruffs, *Philomachus pugnax,* at Malltraeth Field pools, September 2nd to 10th, 1945.

43 Black-tailed godwit, *Limosa limosa*, feeding, Glan Avon, September 1944.

Stroking its bill with
its middle claw.

His white tip not
always present in imm.
birds seen → today

May 4. Fowl Ferry.
Heron perched on side
rail of the ferry causeway.

May 4th. Mrs Wraith Marsh. Haugoffo
Immature Lesser Black Backs. Several
feeding on pasture in company with adult
L.B.Bs. and Herring Gulls.

44

Redshank (First Winter Plumage)
Malltraeth Lake Sept. 15

44 Heron, *Ardea cinerea*, at Foel Ferry and immature lesser black-backed gull, *Larus fuscus*, at Malltraeth, May 4th, 1952.

45 Redshank, *Tringa totanus*, Malltraeth Lake, September 15th, 1946.

May 3rd & 4th.
Small flock of Dunlin on bit Lake. All birds in
bright new plumage, very fresh and clean. A migrating
flock. feeding belly deep by the above.

May 3rd & 4: Common Sandpiper on
shores of Sile Lake. 3 birds. One of the birds
was browner in colour than other two and its eye stripe
was pale buff whereas in the others it was white

46 Dunlin, *Calidris alpina*, in breeding plumage and common sandpipers, *Tringa hypoleucos*, Cob Lake, May 3rd and 4th, 1952.

47 Black-tailed godwits, *Limosa limosa*, and a snipe, *Gallinago gallinago*, Field Pools, Bont Farm, early August, 1948.

48

48 Greenshank, *Tringa nebularia*, at Cob Lake. Wind ruffling feathers. March 27th, 1952.
49 Little stints, *Calidris minuta*, at Cob Lake, September 12th and 13th, 1952.

Little Stints. Bibe Lake. Sept. 12-13.
Either a pair or a single bird seen at intervals
for some days. When feeding with Dunlin did not
rise with the flock but
keep on the margin
of it.

Feather shaking

On Sept. 16 this pale bird
appeared with two others.

Jan 8th Llandwyn,
Purple Sandpiper on rock
below lighthouse.
Feeding on the rocks with
great waves sending
spray over them.

A head bird

In a poor light
these two white spots
on back are apparent.
(noted on all birds seen)

Sometimes
will rest on tarsi
and slide down a
sloping rock

50

50 Studies of purple sandpipers, *Calidris maritima*, at Llandwyn Lighthouse, January 8th, 1950.
51 Bar-tailed godwits, *Limosa lapponica*, at Iona, September 24th, 1934.

Sept. 24ᵗ IONA.   Godwit.   On tide edge feeding with Oyster-Catchers.
In small numbers 5 or 6

In size slightly less than Oyster catcher
which bullies them from their feeding.

51

52 Pair of curlew, *Numenius arquata*, feeding on rough pasture, Goldsitch Moss, April 14th, 1947.

53 Studies of young spoonbill, *Platalea leucorodia*, Foryd estuary, October 15th, 1950.

54

54 Immature heron, *Ardea cinerea*, swallowing a flatfish, Shorelands, November 14th, 1947.

55 Curlew sandpiper, *Calidris ferruginea,* at Malltraeth Pool, August 31st, 1945.

May 12th London Zoo

Bird in foreground with less contrast of black and white especially on back and inner secondaries

(More poses in rough note-book)

56

56 Avocets, *Recurvirostra avosetta*, at London Zoo, May 12th, 1949.
57 Lapwings, *Vanellus vanellus*, at Redesmere, March 12th, 1939.

58 Bar-tailed godwits, *Limosa lapponica*, threatening, Malltraeth Field Pool, August 2nd, 1948.

Geese, Ducks and Swans

32 Grey lags grazing in a marshy field. Jan 4th 51

59 Grey lag, *Anser anser*, grazing in a marshy field, January 4th, 1951.

Barnacle Goslings. From sketches made on July 27th. Kendal.

60 Barnacle goslings, *Branta leucopsis*, from sketches made at Kendal, July 27th, 1944.

61 Pair of gadwall, *Anas strepera*, Cemlyn Lake, March 15th, 1951.

One goose had a peculiar kind of sepia fawn down at the back of the upper neck.

Oct. 29ᵗ Redesmere. Part of a flock of 32 Canadas resting in the shallows of the mere. They were not afloat but were standing on the bottom. Water silvery grey into subtle dark grey ripples causing the reflections of geese and trees to become elongated. Geese were exquisite against the grey background. Lightest part was the top of the breast which became a shade of lilac grey below and at the side becoming pale grey-brown darkening to sepia at the end of flanks. Backs were a soft brown the pale edges of feathers not apparent unless one looked for them.

Flock of 32

62

62 Canada geese, *Branta canadensis*, at Redesmere, October 29th, 1944.
63 Grey lag, *Anser anser*, in wing moult, Y Felin, July 12th, 1952.

64 Studies of bill markings in Bewick's swans, *Cygnus columbianus*, Malltraeth Lake,
February 24th, 1946.

65 Domestic goose, *Anser domesticus*, August 1942.

66 Flying great crested grebe, *Podiceps cristatus*, and (below) coot chick, *Fulica atra*, Redesmere,
June 9th, 1938.

June 9th
Redmere.

Grebe (Adult) flying.
Legs and feet very conspicuous
trailing behind. Wing beats rapid.

Slow to land.

Blush scarlet

Scarlet

P. tip

Ginger down on a darker base.

Pale down

Young Coot.
June 9th.
Redmere.

When the light is
behind the bird the
beak looks semi-
transparent and the
tip dark (probably
denser at the tip)
but when the light
is on the beak the tip
is pale.

A brood of 4 being fed by
the parent birds on what looked
like young, tender water lily shoots.

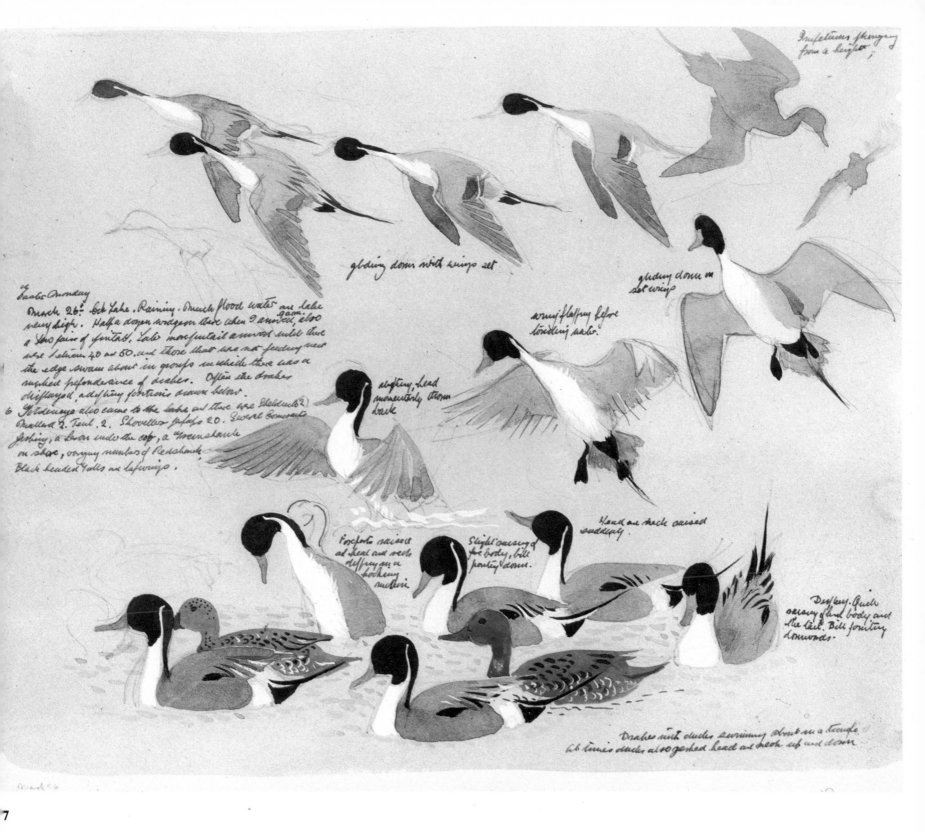

67 Pintails, *Anas acuta*, at Cob Lake, Easter Monday, March 26th, 1951.

First position when alarmed →

2nd position ↓

Younger Geese have not nearly such a large knob and no orange showing ←

Chinese Geese. Nov. 24

Bradley Hall. Mr Clitheroe

68

Red breasted Goose. Zoo. May 22nd.

70

68 Domestic Chinese goose, *Anser cygnoides*, Bradley Hall, near Clitheroe, November 24th, 1934.

69 Red-breasted geese, *Branta ruficollis*, at London Zoo, May 22nd, 1952.

70 Studies of Bewick's swans, *Cygnus columbianus*, taking off and landing, Malltraeth Lake, February 1946.

71 Domestic goose, *Anser domesticus*, August 1942.

Wing stretching.

Sometimes the wing is brought back so that its inner secondaries are covering tail, rump and part of the other wing. This the wing is usually held a little apart from the body whilst in the stretching position but is not in any way opened

The two cobs approaching each other necks back wings dropped and plumes raised. Slowly unhurried walk.

the first flurry, each tries to fasten onto the neck of the other. One succeeds and attempts to press the other to the ice

loosing his grip on neck he loops his own neck over back of opponent and presses down. Eventually he manages to grip his opponents neck, gets on top of him and presses down until his opponents neck and head are flat on ice

Later they break away and the chase and the struggles goes on from place to place on the ice. At times they run over the ice at others they are just air-borne and when coming onto the ice they skid for yards before coming to a standstill.

Often on coming to rest the birds seemed too exhausted to stand up. At intervals the rest of the families approached the fighting birds but did not take part in the fighting.

Landing on ice they skid along on their feet and tails

Redesmere. Jan 21st 46

72 Further studies of the domestic goose, including wing-stretching, August 1942.
73 Male swans, *Cygnus olor*, fighting, Redesmere, January 21st, 1946.

74 Muscovy ducklings, *Cairina moschata*, Northwich, Cheshire, June 30th, 1947.

75 Mallard drake, *Anas platyrhynchos,* Serpentine, London and (below) pintail drake, *Anas acuta,*
at London Zoo, May 11th, 1938.

Mallard. Serpentine & Priory St

Pintail. Zoo

New dark feathers here.

Rest of scapulars very faded, almost silvery.

Aug 27th Young Sheld duck on focile of 18 on Cob Lake.

76 Young shelduck, *Tadorna tadorna*, at Cob Lake, August 8th, 1951.

TY GWYN. May 26th   Shelduck on the Green Marsh.

...duck on the marsh in pairs. Often one of the pair would be feeding in the shallow
...ls while the other would stand by as if on guard. There was some display consisting of
...d and neck movement. Head and neck alternately
...tched vertically and then curved until bill touched
...hrust out chest.

Frequently flew short distances about the marsh, the pair keeping
close.

77 Shelduck, *Tadorna tadorna*, on the Green Marsh, Ty Gwyn, May 26th, 1945.

78 Composition study of the white domestic goose, August, 1942.

79 Domestic geese, *Anser domesticus*, at Malltraeth Marsh, September 8th, 1944.

Shelduck _Traeth Bach May 28th_

Duck much duller in colour than drake
This male had a very small knob on bea

SHELDUCK.
LADIE FOWLS. Welsh.

80 Shelduck, *Tadorna tadorna* (female in foreground), Traeth Bach, May 28th, 1945.

81 Mallard, *Anas platyrhynchos*, at Redesmere, February 9th, 1946.

Birtles Pool · March 5th. Canada pair on the ice and frozen mud. Birds in very immaculate plumage. Dead growth behind is – rushes and tall Willow herb.

82 Canada geese, *Branta canadensis*, at Birtles Pool, March 5th, 1946.

Capesthorne Pool, Sept. 8th Very warm afternoon.
Geese sleepy and rested with heads back.
Bright sunlight. Geese in reflection of yellow, brown
and green reeds. Slight ripple on the water. Fresh
green of lily-leaves (yellow lily) Some reared out of
the water. Geese very sepia in colour.

83 Canada geese, *Branta canadensis*, resting at Capesthorne Pool, September 8th, 1942.
84 Studies of the great crested grebe, *Podiceps cristatus*, and young, Redesmere, July 1935.
85 Drake mallard, *Anas platyrhynchos*, sequence of moult, Gawsworth Pool, July/August 1935.

84

Mallard Drake in
eclipse P.   July 1st   Yansworth Pool.

Both these stages seen on the same
day.

July 1st

Later stage of moult

Fairly early stage of moult

July 1st
(1)

Had the beginnings of the white
ring on neck as a thin line
round the front of the neck.
(not seen in this posit.)

(2)

Aug 18th

(3)   Aug 4th

Lower Breast of this bird a partly grey with
undefinate pinky brown, crescent markings on the outer sides.

(4)   Aug 4th

aug 8° Cob Lake. Juvenile Shelduck strong on
the wing, and without accompanying parents

86

86 Juvenile shelduck, *Tadorna tadorna,* at Cob Lake, August 27th, 1949.

87 Family of Bewick's swans, *Cygnus columbianus*, Malltraeth Lake, February 20th, 1946.

Barnacle Family at Mrs Abbott's, Sawmill Lane, Kendal.
From drawings made July 27th.
Goslings Hatched July 14th. Nest made on the edge of a quarry cliff. Parent birds are birds which were winged by Mrs Abbott on wild-fowling expeditions.

88

88 Barnacle geese, *Branta leucopsis*, and goslings, Kendal, July 1944.

Feb 15ᵗʰ. Llyn Coron.

Water swarming with duck, chiefly Wigeon, with Shoveller
Teal, Tufted, Pochard. Big majority Wigeon, the drakes whistling
so that the place was full of their calls. One excited group of
one duck and five drakes sped over the water this way and
that and when the duck came down to the surface other
drakes joined the group and at one time she was chased
by eight or nine drakes.

Sometimes the duck would
suddenly change direction and seemed
to cut through the group of pursuing
drakes.

Sweeping up in a
glide

attitude when swimming
about calling. The drake
seemed to display a larger fat b
palette on wing than normal

occasionally this attitude
was adopted by a drake when the
company alighted

89 Wigeon, *Anas penelope,* at Llyn Coron, February 15th, 1951.

90

July 6th. Redesmere.
Moorhen with young among water lilies
She with wings much crooked and held
high. Fed the young with bits from the flowers
and also from tearing things from the leaves

90 Moorhen, *Gallinula chloropus*, with chick, Redesmere, July 6th, 1945.

Birds of Prey

Aug 13th. Shorelands.

Juvenile Little Owl.

Brought in a paper bag
by two boys from Capel Manor.
Could not fly when it came to
us. Fed on rabbit and dead
birds. Aug 15th strong on the
wing and very fit.

Pose adopted when ready to fly off perch.
Often with a bobbing up and down of head and neck.

91 Studies of a juvenile little owl, *Athene noctua*, hand-reared by the artist, Shorelands,
August 13th, 1951.

91

Light was so bad could not see if there were any bars or spots in mantle. Feb 4th. Later iriset slowed that mantle was devoid of markings as was the hind crown and nape.

Hissing when I approached close to the cage. On a previous occasion it was housed in a cage next to that of some lion cubs and whenever a cub approached the partition between them Snowy hissed fiercely

92 Snowy owl, *Nyctea scandiaca,* at Chester Zoo, January 29th–February 9th, 1946.
93 Snowy owl, *Nyctea scandiaca,* at Chester Zoo, possibly a young male, January 29th, 1946.
94 Gyr falcon, *Falco rusticolus,* owned by Ronald Stevens, August 1951.
95 Female sparrowhawk, *Accipiter nisus,* on the garden wall, Shorelands, September 1st, 1949.

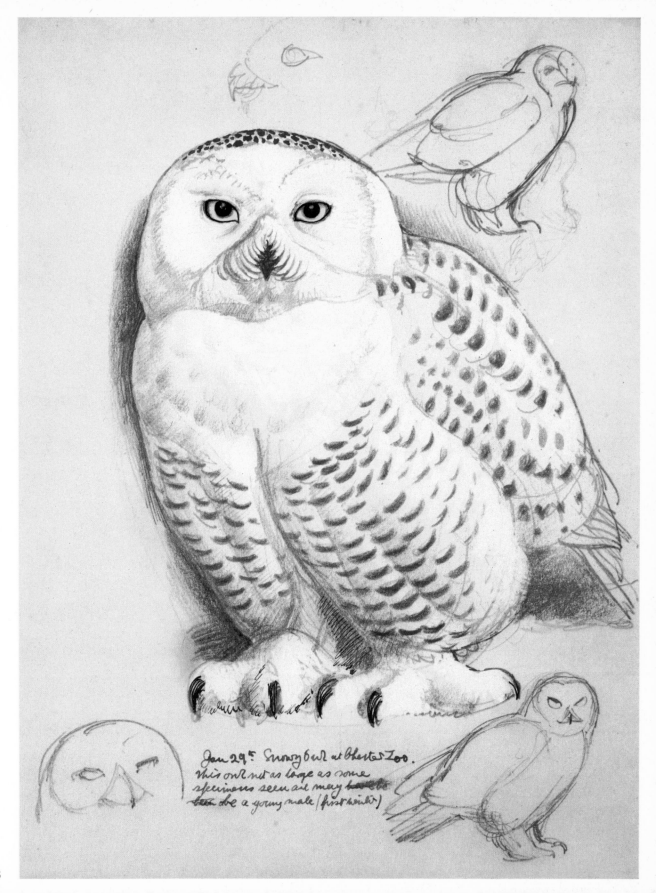

Jan 29th. Snowy Owl at Chester Zoo.
This owl not as large as some
specimens seen and may have been
been be a young male (first winter)

Gyr Falcon owned by Ronald Stevens
Mid August.

Sept 1st Evening.
Sparrow Hawk on the
garden wall. Rested
for some minutes on the wall
near the kitchen door. No
other birds to be seen.
N.B. Flights were held at the
sides of the tail not
above it.

96 Peregrine falcon, *Falco peregrinus*, South Stack, Holy Island, July, probably 1948.

Falcon resting on cliff.
Her back feathers beginning to
look bleached in a little cloudy.

"Tough guy" pose of falcon
just after alighting.

Tiercel perched on a clump of
thrift growing from the
sheer face of the cliff. He
rested here for at least two hours
during the morning of July 12ᵗʰ.

July 12ᵗʰ.

Falcon cleaning
her bill. Cleans
each side alternately
with a side to side
motion of her head.

97 Peregrines, *Falco peregrinus*, at South Stack; the tiercel (left) and falcon, July, probably 1948.

Falcon feeding ey...
One much more advan...
in fledgery than the
other.

98

98 Female ('falcon') peregrine, *Falco peregrinus*, with eyasses, South Stack. June 30th, probably 1948.
99 Study of Ken Williams' Turumti (red-headed) falcon, *Falco chiquera, c.* 1962.
100 & 101 Young sparrowhawks, *Accipiter nisus*, at Hawks-head Clough, July 15th, 1947.
102 Study of a barn owl, *Tyto alba*, autumn 1934.

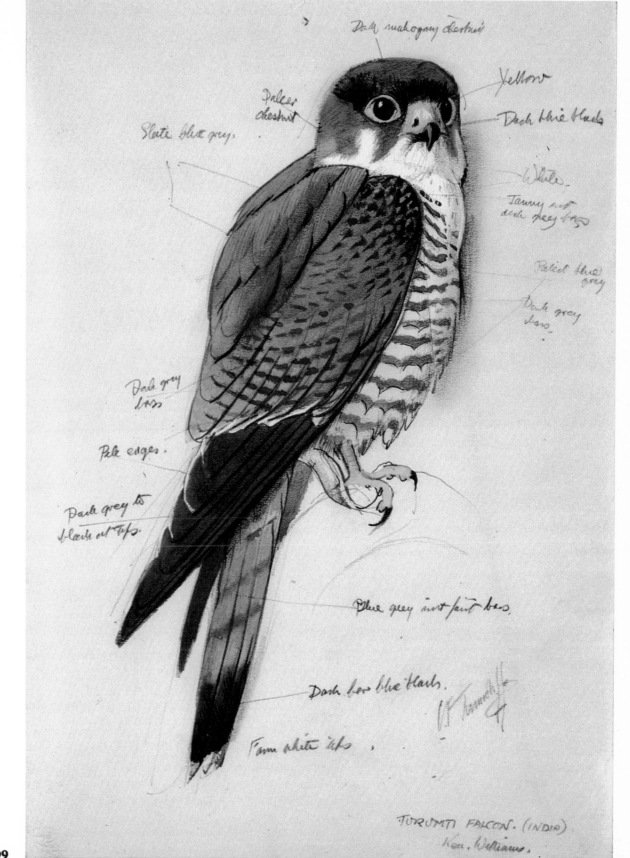

Dark mahogany chestnut

Paler chestnut

Slate blue grey.

Yellow

Dark blue black

White.

Tawny and dark grey base

Palid blue grey

Dark grey bars.

Dark grey bars

Pale edges.

Dark grey to black at tips.

Blue grey and faint bars.

Dark bar blue black.

Faint white tips .

TURUMTI FALCON. (INDIA)
Ken. Williams.

Miscellaneous Birds

The Ring Plover often rested
on a hollow of the weed so
that their legs were hidden.

The group was more spread out
and not so evenly placed as above.

Turnstones were throwing the seaweed over.

Sept. 7th.
Dinas Point.

Ring Plover and Turnstones.
Some young birds among the
R. Plover. Legs of young much
paler than adult, chest mark browner
and not complete. No black above the
eye.

103 Group of adult and immature ringed plovers, *Charadrius hiaticula,* with turnstones,
Arenaria interpres, behind, Dinas Point, September 7th, 1944.

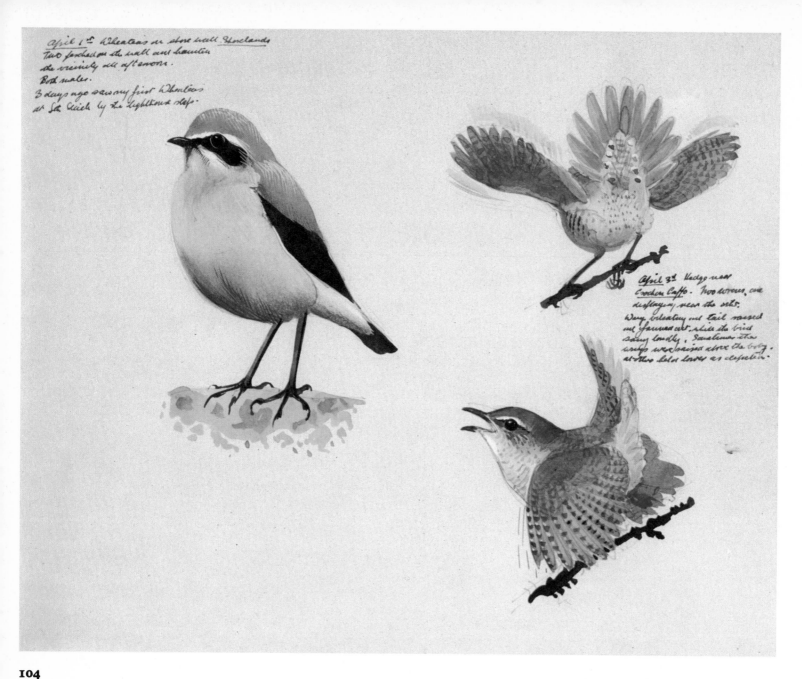

104 An early wheatear, *Oenanthe oenanthe*, at Shorelands, and wrens, *Troglodytes troglodytes*, at Crochan Caffo, April, 1951.

105 Singing wren, *Troglodytes troglodytes*, wren collecting nesting material and (below) wood warbler, *Phylloscopus sibilatrix*, and willow warbler, *Phylloscopus trochilus*, May 13th, 1947.

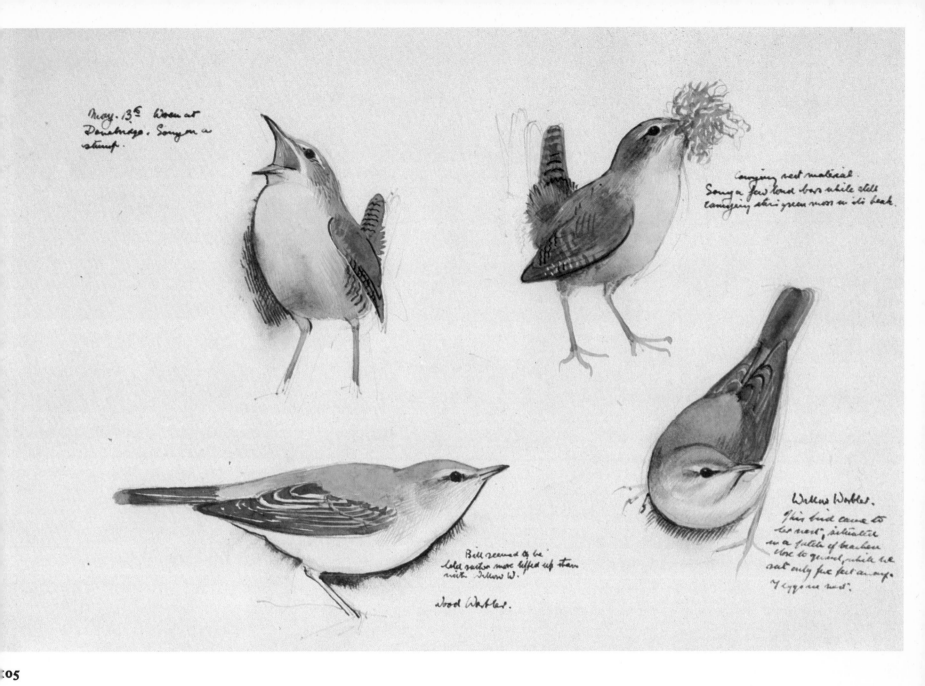

106 A cock green woodpecker, *Picus viridis,* with two juveniles at Shorelands, July 25th, 1951.

107 Female great spotted woodpecker, *Dendrocopos major,* Chester Zoo, August 3rd, 1939.

108 Young jay, *Garrulus glandarius,* study from a dead bird, July 6th and 7th, 1934.

109 Notes from a day at South Stack, March 10th, 1952.

Irides in juvenile
appear dull brown
and in most lights
the eye appears dark.

Shovelands. July 25th.
An adult cock and
two young Green Woodpeckers perched on the short wall, 8 ± 9 am.
Later all flew down to concrete paving and began to feed
in the cracks between the flat stones.
Adult called intermittently as if to keep the young near her.
A high-pitched clear note repeated about 3 times per second
Call of juveniles rather reedy and throaty, not quite so high as adult.

Adult wing
stretching

Young Jay. (from dead bird) July 6th ♂

Blue feathers on the wing not so definately
marked with black & white as in adult bird.
Also head neck and back browner

Length when stretched out about 12".

March 10th Soth Stack. From the lighthouse steps, and looking through the hole in the rock, saw two Fulmars resting on the ledges and also saw another flying about the cliff. Near them a group of Guillemots (8) also noted on the ledges and in the same vicinity a few groups of 2 and 3 Guillemots. While we watched they all left the cliff as if alarmed at our scrutiny. Razorbills were seen flying about the cliffs and over the water but none rested on the cliffs.

Later a Peregrine flew out from the cliffs beyond Helen's Tower and as we climbed the steps a pair of Ravens flew about the cliffs. In a triangular niche in the cliff was a pile of nest material and I thought I detected new material in the cup (this the site of a previous Raven's nest)

All the previous year's guano had been washed from the cliffs.

There were about 30 Fulmars on the ledges when we arrived.

Herring Gulls were dotted about the cliffs in pairs as if they had already staked out their claims for nesting sites

Later we climbed the slip and went down the headlands by Helen's Tower. On the way down watched a cock Stonechat singing on a rock. As he sang he moved his tail up and down, and his throat throbbed as he sang. Furze was coming into flower, careful well out though on its seaward side it was very brown as if it had been burnt — the result of salt-laden gales I suppose.

Looking from the cliff edge down to the sea we saw a solitary Shag swimming. In previous years a solitary pair has nested near the foot of these cliffs.

Moving along the cliff path a Peregrine again went out from the cliff calling loudly. It flew about and glided for a time then turned in the headland and disappeared over the skyline.

Near the place where the great cliffs jut out almost at right angles to the general line a pair of Ravens left the cliff and flew about suspiciously, but here we could find no sign of a nest. Later they returned and flew round again, but we still failed to find a nest or sign of one.

When we returned to Helen's Tower a Peregrine flew out from the cliff opposite, again calling, and after circling away over the sea and the lighthouse came into the cliff again, but this bird rested out of sight in the cliff opposite the steps. While in flight it was several times mobbed by herring gulls but easily eluded them.

110 Goldfinch, *Carduelis carduelis*, feeding young at Shorelands, September 19th, 1949.

Mid aft.
Oct 15ᵗʰ '51 Hoopoe.
First seen flying
up from the drive. It
flew to the shore and
settled to feed on the
little saltings, thrusting
its bill vertically down.
then it flew to a stone
and rested for a time before
flying off over the bungalow

Resting on a stone.

Feeding.

alert and ready to fly.

III Hoopoe, *Upupa epops*, at Shorelands, October 1951.

Aug. 14ᵗʰ Clough Brook, Wildboarclough.
Cock Grey Wagtail in moult.
Outer tail feathers half-grown.
Remains of black throat still visible.
Some inner secondaries missing.

When preening, dropped wings
so that lower back and rump
are visible.

112 Cock grey wagtail, *Motacilla cinerea*, in moult, Clough Brook, August 14th, 1944.
113 Juvenile long-tailed tit, *Aegithalos caudatus*, Radnor Mere, June 26th, 1939.

Looks very
filling when at ease

Wheatear on the side of bag of
Body movement feeding in wood. April 28th

June 9th Cob Lake Shore.

Feeding

115

114 Studies of a cock wheatear, *Oenanthe oenanthe*, Bosley Reservoir, April 28th, 1938.
115 A ruff, *Philomachus pugnax*, in breeding plumage, Cob Lake, June 9th, 1949.

116 Cuckoo, *Cuculus canorus*, on barbed wire, April 1946.

March 13th Redesmere.
Small company of Redpolls - 6 or 7 birds.
feeding on the alders at the side of
mere. Sometimes they dropped to the
ground and searched among dead leaves
and plants and grasses.   Day of cold wind

One hen observed was a very
grey bird with very pronounced
light wing bars.

117 Redpolls, *Acanthis flammea,* on an alder branch, Redesmere, March 13th, 1946.

Man ark at Alderley Edge:

Aug. 22nd   "Greenfinch feeding young.

Young are constantly calling and flapping half-open wings. Food is thrust into the bill of young by parent who seems to regurgitate as no food was visible in her bill before she fed the young.

118 Greenfinch, *Carduelis chloris*, feeding young, Alderley Edge, August 22nd, 1944.
119 Spotted flycatcher, *Muscicapa striata*, with young, Gawsworth, July 11th, 1944.

April 6ᵗʰ Radnor Woods. '47. Gt. Sp. Woodpecker.

120

120 Great spotted woodpecker, *Dendrocopos major*, Radnor Woods, April 6th, 1947.
121 Cock chaffinch, *Fringilla coelebs*, at Redesmere, March 9th, 1939.